Sex Positions for Couples

A beginner's guide to explore the best sex positions and increase the passion you feel for each other to have a mind-blowing sex life.

By

Richard Tips

Legal & Disclaimer

The information contained in this book and its contents is not designed to replace or take the place of any form of medical or professional advice; and is not meant to replace the need for independent medical, financial, legal or other professional advice or services, as may be required. The content and information in this book has been provided for educational and entertainment purposes only.

The content and information contained in this book has been compiled from sources deemed reliable, and it is accurate to the best of the Author's knowledge, information and belief. However, the Author cannot guarantee its accuracy and validity and cannot be held liable for any errors and/or omissions. Further, changes are periodically made to this book as and when needed.

Where appropriate and/or necessary, you must consult a professional (including but not limited to your doctor, attorney, financial advisor or such other professional advisor) before using any of the suggested remedies, techniques, or information in this book.

Upon using the contents and information contained in this book, you agree to hold harmless the Author from and against any damages, costs, and expenses, including any legal fees potentially resulting from the application of any of the information provided by this book. This disclaimer applies to any loss, damages or injury caused by the use and application, whether directly or indirectly, of any advice or information presented, whether for breach of contract, tort, negligence, personal injury, criminal intent, or under any other cause of action.

You agree to accept all risks of using the information presented inside this book.

You agree that by continuing to read this book, where appropriate and/or necessary, you shall consult a professional (including but not limited to your doctor, attorney, or financial advisor or such other advisor as needed) before using any of the suggested remedies, techniques, or information in this book.

Table of Contents

Introduction 7

Chapter 1: Using Your Environment and Other Inanimate Objects to Your Advantage 13

Chapter 2: Vitamins and Lifestyle Changes That Help Your Sex Drive 21

Chapter 3: Great Sexual Positions for Her 28

Emotional positions 28

Chapter 4: Great Sexual Positions for Him 38

Chapter 5: Change of Scenery 66

Chapter 6: The Other "Naughty" Places 70

Chapter 7: Sensual Massage 74

Chapter 8: Fantasy 77

Chapter 9: A few Décor tweaks 80

The tantra chair 81

Love Bumpers 83

Swings, slings and Hammocks 85

Chapter 10: Mr. Romance 88

Setting the scene 90

Food as orgasm Booster 93

Get Sensual 95

Let the games begin 97

The dance if Love 98

Chapter 11: A Little Bit Risqué................................ 101

Conclusion 134

Introduction

If you are married or living in happily unwedded bliss, you and your partner have sex. If you do not have sex, then you need more help than this book can give you. However, chances are high that you are at least having pretty decent sex, and occasionally, even having rowdy bedroom sessions. So, let's get serious, and talk about it. Sex is an important part of a relationship. It does not matter if you have been married for 15 years or dating for 6 months. Any professional therapist will tell you the same – sex is an essential part of every successful relationship. Sex is more than just two bodies mating in hopes of creating life. If that was all sex was good for, then why in the world is it so damn enjoyable?

Why is sex so important to a relationship? After all, the two of you have found a connection, have created a bond, and are content with each other. Who cares if your burning loins tend to lean more towards a low simmer? Why should it matter if the sex starts to fade in both quality and quantity? It matters. It matters a lot. Sex in relationships is more than just two people dancing in the sheets for the sheer pleasure of it. It is more than the path to procreation. Sex in a relationship is part of the way you create intimacy; it is a way of staying connected with each other even if miles are separating you. After all, in day-to-day life, there are so many other things going on – kids, school, work, bills, errands – it is way too easy to come home and forgo sex. Even on a slow weekend, it can still be too easy to say, "Not tonight, dear," as you roll back over to your Kindle to finish your book.

The problem with this is skipping intercourse also means skipping the connection that comes with sex. It also becomes much easier to make it a habit to skip the sex in favor of a good Netflix documentary or an extra 30 minutes in the bathtub. Of course, people must take care of themselves and their mental and physical health. But you cannot ignore the mental and physical health of the relationship – and it does have a mind of its own. There is a level of intimacy between two people in a relationship that is absent in the casual dating scene. That intimacy has to be nourished throughout the length of the marriage or relationship. Two people cannot just live together and raise kids and pay bills while ignoring their sex life. The loss of intimacy will, inevitably, lead to the loss of the relationship.

Couples need a sexual connection. Women need the emotional intimacy that comes from foreplay, sex, and pillow talk. Men need physical intimacy that comes from sex. It is definitely true that men and women are wired differently when it comes to the act of intercourse. But the result is the same – they both finish having sex and feel closer, bonded, and emotionally and sexually satisfied. Now, men might not like to own up to feeling these emotions and bonds and connections. After all, big, strong men aren't supposed to be complex, emotional creatures. But the truth is that both men and women get not only physical satisfaction from sex; they also get emotional fulfillment. Couples need to separate their regular lives as individuals from their sex life as partners. It does not matter how many hours you had to sit through a boring meeting at work. It does not matter how stressful your partner's visit to his parents' home was for him. When the two of you come home at night, you are doing more than just coming into a home. You are coming home to each other. When you let the normal stuff take control of your life, when you let the stress and tension and worry occupy your mind, keeping sexual needs at bay, your relationship will suffer.

That is why sex is so great and amazing for a relationship! Sex brings two people (or in some instances, more than two people) together – literally! Once two bodies are entwined together in a tangle of sheets and desire, the rest of the world is easy to forget. For those 5-minute quickies or those hours-long "sexathons," the dishes do not matter; the kids are tucked out of sight and out of mind; the pile of laundry is forgotten, and the focus is on each other. Sex is not only good for your mind, but it is also good for your body. There are just so many almost magical things that happen inside of you both every time you come together and make love. The afterglow that comes from a rousing round of intense sex eases your mind, relieves your stress, and helps you fall into a deep and restful sleep. If couples fail to focus on each other sexually, how can they possibly focus on each other emotionally?

Sex brings two people in a relationship closer together. Not just in a physical sense, although you really cannot get much physically closer than a little afternoon delight. Sex brings two people closer mentally and emotionally. Think about it: you are literally at your most vulnerable. You are naked for your partner to see all of your perceived flaws. So, when the two of you come together in the most intimate of ways, there is a level of trust, love, and security that is only heightened by the sexual experience. You are standing before your partner, and he before you, and you are both silently asking for acceptance. The act of sex is a reassuring way to make sure your partner knows that you still feel desire, that you still want him in an almost animalistic way, that you have a physical need to feel him as close to you as possible – deep inside of you. In a relationship, sex is much more than just physical pleasure. It is an emotional connection wrapped around physical satisfaction.

That's not to say that pleasure is not involved – of course, it is. Sex is a pleasure. It releases certain chemicals in the brain that make you feel just as fantastic on the inside as you do on the outside. In a relationship, there is definitely a time for pure, physical sex – just fulfilling a raw, primal need. There are going to be days when you come home and the only thing on your mind is being bent over the back of the couch like the bad girl you are. There are going to be days when you will be standing in the kitchen, minding your own business, and your partner takes it upon himself to have his way with you. It is good to feel this wanted and desired, especially after years in a relationship. So, whether you are making love with your partner or simply satisfying a sexual craving, sex is obviously essential to the continued strength of your relationship. You both need the connection, the intimacy, the heat, the passion, the release – sex makes a relationship stronger. Any and all healthy relationships include a great sex life. But what if you are not in a relationship? Is sex still an important part of your life as a single person? Absolutely.

Chapter 1: Using Your Environment and Other Inanimate Objects to Your Advantage

The use of toys while performing sexual acts has now become quite normal for couples.

Examples of sex toys are:

Vibrators – These come in many shapes and sizes and are used for clitoral stimulation through a vibrating device. The intensity of the vibrations can also be modified.

Dildos – These are representations of the penis and, depending on the manufacturer, can come in the form of an anatomically correct appendage or a sleek conical rod.

Vibrating Dildos – As the name suggests, these gadgets are combinations of vibrators and the dildos.

Synthetic vagina – The popularity of the modified use of the penis pump has resulted in the creation of the synthetic vagina. This gadget is basically a penis pump with a synthetic material stretched over the main opening simulating the real thing. This is where the penis is inserted and then the device is used as a masturbatory tool using the hand's manual motions. Because there is a different sensation other than the hand, it is an effective masturbatory tool. Due to popular demand, the synthetic mouth and synthetic anus were created and they simulate their respective namesakes.

Sex dolls – These are representations of a real person and come in various shapes and sizes. Some are plain rubber inflatable dolls with the right orifices or appendages to simulate a real person or are more sophisticated and lifelike in appearance like the ones seen in more recent sex industry conventions.

These items are included in this book because they can be used as sexual aids to increase the level of sexual stimulation during coitus.

Stairway to Heaven

This Led Zeppelin-inspired sexual act has nothing to do with the band. Instead, it is focused on including the use of stairs in the sexual act. The normal execution for this act is to have the man seated on the steps of the staircase and the woman on top while supporting her on the handrails as she goes up and down and controls the level of stimulation.

The rise in popularity of this sexual position is because couples sometimes do not reach the actual bedroom in their hurry to engage in sexual activities.

The Spin Cycle

Another commonplace that sexual activity can take place is in the laundry room. This has given rise to the Spin Cycle.

What this basically requires is for the woman to sit on the edge of a washing machine as she is penetrated by the man standing in front of her. The added mechanical vibration can induce orgasms. The

16

washing machine basically becomes an oversized vibrator in operation and concept.

Swiss Ball Blitz

One of the things first discussed in this book was the importance of keeping fit. Now, what if you could keep fit AND have sex at the same time?

This sexual position requires the use of a stability or exercise ball. With the man sitting on the ball, the woman can then sit with her back to him and then control the thrusts by pumping down. The ball will then react by bouncing back with each thrust and depending on the intensity of each thrust can give the impression that the man is ramming hard into the vagina.

The Countertop

This is best performed with a sturdy platform for the woman to lie on. The man is standing as the woman lies down on her back with her pelvic region off of the table or the countertop. Her pelvis is supported by the man as he thrusts into her with her legs raised or bent at the knee. To avoid getting knocked off of the platform, the woman can hold on to the sides of the table as powerful thrusts are given by the man.

Couch Surfer

This is perfect for sexual activities outside of the bedroom.

The woman bends over the couch and is entered from behind by the man. She can then use the couch for tactile stimulation by grinding against it while the man penetrates her. This is a very erotic position and is high on the list of couples for sexual positions to try outside of the bedroom.

H2O Yeah

If you are the adventurous type and like having sex in public, this is one of the most discreet ways to do it. First, you'll need a pool, though.

You'll have to enter her from behind and the water will take care of the rest.

The good thing about this position is you won't need to strip down completely naked. Prying away parts of the lower part of her swimsuit and yours will strategically hide your privates from the general public.

Drop the Soap

Sometimes a woman just wants to get dirty while getting cleaned at the same time.

This position is ideal when done in the proper atmosphere which is the toilet and bath. This is done by letting the woman hold on to the bathroom walls while she is entered by the man from behind. The additional stimulus provided by the cascading water from the shower will add to sexual pleasure.

This can also be done as a quickie while at a party. That is without the obvious water stimulation of course and without having to strip completely naked to perform this. This variation is aptly called "Drop the Soap" as that can be your excuse when other people find out that you've been up to something naughty inside the cubicle!

Chapter 2: Vitamins and Lifestyle Changes That Help Your Sex Drive

In the last chapter, we covered bases on things that you can do to make yourself ready for great sex, but there is help from the vitamin field as well that you may benefit from. If you are finding that you cannot last that long when you make love, you may want to consider some of these alternatives as they really will help you to have sex for longer. They do need to be taken regularly to have effective results, but the list within this chapter will be helpful to those who feel that sex should be better than it actually is.

Citrulline – Although you may not be aware of this, this vitamin comes from the melon family and has been used for stamina for years. It isn't just used by people who want to increase the length of time that they can make love. It's also used by gymnasts and people who simply want to up their exercise so it will serve two purposes. Citrulline is nature's answer to

Viagra, so if you would rather not discuss your love life with your doctor, you can buy supplements of L-citrulline, but always respect the dosage as mentioned on the pack. Taking more of it won't improve your performance. It's not a bad supplement to take in general because it will also up your energy and that may just be what you need to feel great and to have sufficient energy at night to be sure of having a good time in bed.

Vitamin E is also a great vitamin to extend your love life into your later years. If you are middle-aged and find that your libido is sinking fast, this is a good vitamin to take as it will help lift you out of that period toward feeling much more like having sex. Since vitamin E has many benefits both for men and for women, it's a little bit of a sneaky vitamin because you don't even have to mention that you are taking it to get your sex life into check! Popeye ate spinach for a purpose and eating spinach can also increase your intake of vitamin E.

Phenylalanine – This is something that is found in peanuts and all sorts of different foods such as almonds and pineapples. It is known as an aphrodisiac and if you are not eating these foods, you can buy supplements and take them daily. A daily dosage amount will depend upon the supplements that you purchase, so do respect the instructions given on the packet. Look also at contra-indications since you may be producing sufficient phenylalanine yourself and may not need it.

Magnesium, Zinc and Folic Acid – These are normally derived from your food, but you can buy vitamin tablets that will help the levels. Folic acid is important if you are trying for a baby since this can strengthen the sperm count.

The best way forward is to make sure that you have a varied diet and that it includes foods that produce all the vitamins and minerals that your body needs.

Lifestyle changes

One of the biggest problems when it comes to sex life is lack of sleep. You may think that people who don't sleep have more sex, but their bodies are unable to heal correctly. Sleep is essential to help all of the organs to regenerate and to heal after a day of work and it's vital that you have good quality sleep. If you are a victim of the times and find it hard to get quality sleep, try relaxation classes or even try lying down and listening to a relaxation tape before bedtime because this will help you to achieve the sleep that you need. If you are not getting a decent night's sleep, it will interfere with your sex life and it's important that you address this.

Sleep gives your body the ability to physically and mentally recuperate. Without proper sleep, you will begin to notice difficulties in all aspects of your life. It may not be obvious, but lack of sleep can cause irritability, mood swings, fatigue, aches and pains, and can cause a lot of unnecessary strain on your organs because while you are sleeping, your organs are resting as well. There are a lot of different ways to get your sleep in check. Your last resort should be medication because these have a lot of debilitating side effects and are not ideal to take over long periods of time. It is better to find a long-term solution to your problem by the use of relaxation techniques, meditation, exercise, proper diet, and checkups to make sure everything else is healthy.

Overeating will also meddle with your love life, especially if you eat late at night. This can cause all kinds of problems because the digestion is not able to cope with this amount of food at night and you may find this is a reason why you are not sleeping correctly. Cut down the amount that you eat at night and make sure that you detox occasionally, to keep your digestive tract in good order. A great detox is to drink nettle tea. If you brew a whole pan full at a time and pour this into a plastic water bottle, you can drink it throughout the day and it will help you to detox, making your body feel less sluggish and encouraging you to be more inclined toward wanting sex!

Having energy can create a whole new sex drive you never thought you had. Overeating can hinder this energy so don't eat more than you need to feel full. Also, do not eat right before sex to avoid getting sick, the last thing you want is to get sick in bed. Overeating also leads to weight can which in turn, leads to belly fat. We have already discussed how belly fat can negatively affect your love life.

Drinking water is also important from the male and the female perspective. It helps you to keep your skin smooth and refreshed and it also helps your body to hydrate which will help you to be able to sustain sex for longer. These are habits that you need to employ if you want the best chance possible for your love life to keep going years into the future.

Lowering stress can help you in the bedroom as well. Having high amounts of stress can cause men to have difficulty ejaculating or getting and maintaining an erection. High amounts of stress in a woman can cause her to be unable to climax because of the amount of thoughts and stressors on her mind. A lot of us do not realize the incredible effect on our health that stress has. It causes our muscles to tighten, making it more difficult to relax and get comfortable during sex. Being able to erase all other problems and just focus on sex can be difficult, but trying different outlets like exercise, meditation, yoga, and pilates can all have a positive impact on your life.

Chapter 3: Great Sexual Positions for Her

In this chapter, we are going to go into the positions that are best for her from several viewpoints. For example, if she likes to feel emotional attachment, then the positions that are chosen have been given as examples because they allow that intimacy that is important for a woman. Conversely, she may want a deep experience and this can be achieved by using the positions that are shown later in the chapter.

Emotional positions

These are important from a female point of view because she loves emotional security. A woman is driven by emotions. She needs to feel needed. She doesn't like to be used and certainly will not react well if there is not a little emotion mixed in with other sexual positions. Women like variety, but it is the emotional positions that will really win her over.

In the end, though, most positions can be turned into emotional positions with the use of excessive rubbing, touching, and kissing. For example, entering a woman from behind can feel very empty because you cannot see her face and her reactions. However, by reaching your hands around and cupping her breasts, kissing her back and lower back, and even gently pulling her hair can turn this seemingly shallow position into a position of great intimacy and emotion. You will get out of sex, what you put in, so keep this in mind. You cannot expect certain positions to come off as emotional if you are not willing to put the emotions into the positions.

If your woman is sleeping with her back to you, this is an ideal chance to cuddle up spoon fashion and to hold onto her breasts. She loves skin to skin and this is about as good as it gets. She will also feel if you want sex because this will be obvious and she has the choice of whether to respond or not. Don't expect a response that is favorable every time. Sometimes a cuddle is enough. However, if you don't get too masculine and push yourself on her, she is much more likely to be receptive and even encourage you to move so that you are inside of her.

This position is warm and loving and ideal for mornings when you wake up. It shows a great deal of respect for her and she will respond to it in a very positive way. It's also a great starter position that can easily lead to other positions that maybe even deeper and more passionate. Kissing her gently on the back of the neck and licking her ear lobes can help with arousal if your end goal is penetration. Whispering sweet or dirty phrases and sayings in her ear can help to arouse her as well.

Another emotional position is the reversed missionary because it puts her in control and you get to admire her body at the same time. This is a great position with her seated on top of you and in control. It shows a great deal of trust on the part of the man and he should encourage her to do what she will! What he is accepting when he encourages this position is that he sees her as an equal and that's very important in this day and age. It isn't all about him. It's about both of them and this position says he is open to that kind of thinking.

Crisscross is a wonderful position that allows for easy access to the woman clitoris, usually requiring stimulation to achieve an orgasm. Crisscross is when the woman lies on her back and the man lies beside her on his side. She drapes her legs over him in an "x" position, allowing him to enter her from behind. This also gives him easy access to caress her breasts or kiss her, allowing for deeper connections during sex.

The coital alignment technique is said to be the "greatest sex position in the world" because of the close physical connection and the best clitoral stimulation. This position is started in a normal missionary position but is then transitioned by the man leaning forward and putting all of his weight onto her. He is this supposed to move himself forward until the base of his penis (also known as the pubic bone) is touching her clitoris. The woman then wraps her legs around the man's thighs and they move together in a rocking motion.

The ankles-up position involves the woman being on her back with the man in front, like the missionary position. From here, instead of him leaning forward, he is going to stand straight up and grab each of her ankles with his hands. Holding onto the ankles, he is going to then thrust himself into her. This allows for great depth and a visually stimulating picture for the man.

Positions that will give depth

Several positions give extra depth and if a man is smaller, or worries about his size, then these are probably going to be the best for him as well. If you start with the spoon position and then move so that he is kneeling behind her, this position gives him great access and means that he can get deeper. That means that he will feel more but it also means that he is more likely to reach those places that women really need the man to, to achieve climax.

Using a pillow can also help with deeper penetration and maintaining pleasure. A pillow can either be placed under her stomach while participating in doggy-style, or underneath her lower back when participating in missionary. This elevation provided by the pillow allows for deeper penetration and a great visual for the man as well. There is easy access to the clitoris for either the man or the woman, and both parties have an amazing view of each other.

Another position that is good starts with a missionary position or reversed missionary with either him or her on top. If she is on top, then he rolls her over so that she is beneath him and then moves away a little so that he can grab her legs and place her ankles onto his shoulders. This too is a very deep experience and she will certainly appreciate that because it means that both are satisfied. If you are doing this for the first time, and you are well endowed, take it slowly at first because she may not be accustomed to that depth and it takes a little while to become accustomed to it. Too harsh a movement may hurt her. Remember that her participation is as important as yours. If you are going to try deep sex, then make sure that she is aware of how deep you are going to go. She may, on the other hand, encourage it and pull you toward her so that she takes everything that you have.

Having her bend over and spread her legs apart slightly, allowing him to enter her while he is on his knees behind her, gives a great deal of depth as well. Entering from this position can be done rough or gently depending on the needs and wants of the woman, always enter gently initially to avoid injury.

Having the man sit on the edge of a chair or a solid object, then having the woman sit on his lap facing him provides deep penetration. The woman can take control or she can stand on the balls of her feet and have him take control, whichever the couple prefers. This position can also incorporate a great deal of kissing, making it more passionate, because you are face to face with one another.

A position called the butterfly is done when a woman lies on her back with her legs spread apart. The man is standing and enters her from the front. She then angles her hips upward and places a pillow or a blanket to help keep her hips elevated. The man continues to enter her this way, allowing for maximum penetration.

Shyness

Respect a shy woman and take it slowly. She may have self-image problems and it will take her a while to trust that you love her just the way that she is. Never make her endure being vulnerable. Instead, it is better to encourage nakedness slowly until she reaches a time when it is no longer a problem. Then, you really can explore each other's bodies without inhibitions getting in the way. If you try to take it too quickly in a situation like this, you may frighten her, which may make future lovemaking episodes even more difficult. It's important to gain her trust. You have to appreciate that women are shy for different reasons. Some – it's just a question of body image. With others – they may have experienced something that frightened them in the past and will need your help and understanding to overcome their fears.

Some women are taught that sex is a man's game and to abide by his wants and needs. Some women are taught not to cater to a man's needs in the bedroom, but to instead focus on what each of you has to offer. Being shy in the bedroom can be a mixture of how one was raised along with how comfortable one is in her skin. When dealing with a shy woman, compliment her often and tell her everything you love about her. Tell her she has nothing to be shy about and encourage her. Different women come from different backgrounds. There is no telling what caused her to feel shy about being in the bedroom.

Chapter 4: Great Sexual Positions for Him

You may be surprised that there are positions that are clear leaders both for women and for men, but different reasons. A reverse missionary, with her on top, is actually the number one position for a man. He puts her in control and you may think that men don't like that, but you would be wrong. If she is taking the lead, she is pleasing herself, but she is also freeing up his hands so that he can enjoy her contours. That's important to a man. He can fondle her breasts and enjoy himself and when he wants to take control, it's very easy from this position by simply flipping her over!

A missionary position, although fairly boring if done too often can also be very passionate for a man who likes to take control. He loves the skin to skin contact. It gives him the animal feeling of being in control and that's a natural state for a man to feel good in, especially in bed. Not only that, he can feel her hips pushing toward him and can allow him to pull her toward him so that lips can lock in passion. Some people love that closeness and a man likes to feel he has his woman ready to kiss, to hold, to fondle, and to love and this position gives him it all. It isn't as dull as some may suppose, because it gives a man a lot of thrust. It's an easy position for him to use his full thrust to fill her and to feel her responding to him.

If you are going to do the missionary position, be aware that men hate resistance, and sometimes this is a position that seems to encourage that. You need plenty of foreplay because if he cannot enter you, he will find it frustrating. Thus the foreplay should be encouraged so that there is no difficulty at all entering the vagina. It's also a fallacy that men only like this position because it gives them control. Yes, they do have control, but they also like their woman to move in harmony with them, rather than just lying there letting they do all the work.

In intimate positions such as these, the aroma of the skin is vital to the situation because odors really can put a man off. Make sure that you have bathed. Make your skin soft with oils and also make sure that your breath is superbly fresh. There is nothing worse than a man leaning forward to kiss a woman who smells like last night's ashtray.

Doggie style allows a man to give more thrust and to be in control. This is the position that also gets him deepest inside her. He also gets a great view of her and can see himself entering her vagina, so that this works as a stimulation to make him feel even sexier. How the woman controls the situation is by placing herself in such a position that she gains a little control as well and can tease him a little to make the lovemaking last longer. If he wants her to, she can do as much thrusting as she lives taking in as much of his penis as she feels that she is comfortable with. That makes it a win position for both the man and the woman. The only snag with this position is that it does encourage the man to climax early, so it's better to start in another position and to move into this position for the finale, by which time both man and woman will be ready for that violent thrust and can enjoy joint climaxes if they get it right.

Most men have fantasies about quickies and although this isn't what people should do all of the time, the naughtiness involved in a quickie really will turn him on and drive him crazy. Whether this is against a wall, over a table, or sneaked in when no one is suspecting it, the naughtier the action, the more they turn on. It has to be naughty. It has to be quick and it has to feel good for both. Thus, expect it to be over quickly, but expect it to be both violent and crazy because it will be. This gives a man a great sense of control but it also shows him how naughty his woman is prepared to be.

The 69 position is a favorite for men who love oral sex. It puts both in control of the other's climax and if you go by the old Kama Sutra belief that sex isn't about you, it's about pleasure to your partner – then this position really does work to do that. Both of you are giving each other pleasure. However, there are snags with this position. If she has hair, then perhaps this would put you off, and it may be a good thing to encourage her to remove it, though never encourage this in a way that makes her feel like she is lacking in some way. Introduce the subject and say how you think it would be if she had no hair. Similarly, a woman may not like him climaxing in her mouth and may be shy about it, and in a case such as this, you can turn at the last minute and penetrate her so that the climax happens inside her and you both feel the benefit of it.

Men and women have different preferences because of the way that they are built. The reverse cowboy is favored by some men because he can see her but he can also see himself entering her, which is a great turn on. If you try these positions, you won't go far wrong, and the naughtier the nicer. Men like to know that their women are fully involved in sex and are enjoying it as much as they are.

The following sex positions are recommended for lovers who are already quite experienced. Note that some of these positions are easy to perform while others may require a lot more flexibility, strength, and stamina.

T-Square Position

This is one of the most difficult positions in this book (perhaps the most difficult one) and it is best suited for men with really long penises. It is also a sideward sex position, which means it is quite rarely done in bed. If you are truly adventurous and the man has quite the length to show then you can try this one for size.

How to Do It

The woman will lie on her back. She will then bend her knees as she spreads her legs. The man will then lie on his side perpendicular to the woman (it's like she will be sitting on him if you are viewing the couple from the top).

He then scoots his body underneath her arched or bent legs placing her legs over his hips. He then supports his upper body with one arm and penetrates her from that sideward position (fig. 1).

Fig. 1   T- square position

Pros

- This unusual sex position can be quite interesting for the sexually adventurous.

- It's a relaxing position for the woman since the man does all the work.

- The man has one hand free to reach her breasts for a little fondling.

- This is a great position for guys who are much taller than the girls (works well if you're dating a short petite woman).

Cons

- This position is better suited for guys with longer penises.

- This position can be quite tiring for the guy. It will call for a lot of core strength to swing back and forth.

- This position can get frustrating even after some practice. It takes a lot of stamina and if the guy gets tired too quickly he might even lose his erection.

Sultry Saddle

The woman on top position is a true favorite nowadays. But if you add a little sideways sex variation to it the jolt and pleasure of the experience exponentiates!

How to Do It

The guy lies down in bed. One distinct difference from the usual woman on top position is that his legs will be bent with the knees protruding upwards. Note that his legs should be spread apart a little bit.

The woman then kneels at his right side and then she carefully places her right leg in between the man's legs instead of straddling him with her legs on either side of him. She will then take on a sideward position almost facing his left knee. Still in a kneeling position, she can move her right foot and position it under his left leg (note: she can hold onto his left knee for support and lean against his right knee for balance).

She then takes his cock and inserts it into her. She then rocks back and forth. Note that the woman may have to adjust her position until his cock reaches her G-spot (Fig. 2).

Fig. 2 Sultry saddle position

Pros

- Relatively easy position with the woman being in control.

- Both partners get to experience sex from a totally different angle.

Cons

- The woman will have to make several adjustments to the angle of penetration before she gets to feel that G-spot stimulation. It will take a few tries at first but with some persistence and practice, she will learn how to get things in line for maximum pleasure.

- This sex position will feel awkward at first

Melody Maker

You can call this as one of the best finishing moves in case you've been building things up to the climax. It's your choice if you want to try a rather difficult position in the end or go for something simpler like missionary or any of the basic sex positions mentioned in the first chapter of this book.

There are a few advantages of this position over the basics. First off is that it gives a pretty good angle of penetration that both partners will enjoy. Having said that, the orgasm that both partners will feel will be truly mind-blowing.

They don't call it the "melody maker" for nothing. Both partners will be moaning and groaning as soon as they reach climax in this one.

How to Do It

The woman sits on a footstool or an otherwise comfortable chair. If sitting on a chair then sit sideways so that you can't lean back against the backrest. The woman will then lean back until her head dangles and points down toward the floor.

She then spreads eagle and the man positions himself in between her legs. He holds her hands to give more support and then he enters her. If the chair is too low then the man should kneel.

Pros

- This sex position allows a deeper and more satisfying penetration.

- The woman usually gets a blood rush as she reaches orgasm, which heightens the sensations of the experience.

- It's a relatively easy position for the man since he will be positioned as if in doggy style.

- It's great for men with regular-sized or even smaller sized penises.

Cons

- This position will feel awkward at first especially for the woman who will be trying it for the very first time. Needless to say, the more times you try it the better it feels and the more explosive orgasms you both will get.

The Kneeling Fox

This position sounds like it is one of those positions taken directly out of the Kama Sutra. It's an ideal position for truly well-endowed men. This is a simple variation of the doggy style.

How to Do It

The woman goes on her hands and knees just like in the doggy style. The guy kneels behind the woman as if sitting on his legs with his butt almost touching the bed (as if seated). He then grabs her by the waist and then pulls her back as he eases his cock into her. And now it's the woman who is in control of the pace (Fig. 3).

Fig. 3 Kneeling fox position

Pros

- Gives the initiative back to the woman.

- You can go from standard doggy style then switch to the kneeling fox just to switch control of the action.

- Increased intimacy since the guy has both hands free.

Cons

- Not for guys with smaller size penis. Even some guys with the regular sized ones may have difficulty doing it.

53

- The knees of both partners may get sore if they stay in this position for a prolonged time.

- Not the most romantic sex position but it's one of those that really zero in on the woman's G-spot.

The Spread Eagle on Top

This is a variation of the woman on top position or cowgirl. It basically adjusts the angle of penetration. This sex position also allows the couple to do some really good clitoral stimulation.

How to Do It

The man will lie flat on the bed. The girl will then climb on top. She lowers herself onto him holding his cock for an easy entry. She will then spread her legs open as far out as she can do it. She then rocks back and forth (Fig. 4).

Fig. 4 Spread eagle position

Pros

- Improved angle of penetration compared to women on top.

- The clitoral action also increases the chances of the woman reaching climax.

- The woman is in control.

- The man can enjoy the view as well as the deep penetration.

Cons

- Since the woman's legs are stretched, they can feel numb or painful if the intercourse is prolonged.

Galloping Horse

This is a sit and straddle position but with a little twist. It actually improves the angle of penetration and increases the pleasure level several notches upward. It's a pretty comfortable position for the ladies though it can strain them a little bit.

How to Do It

Just like the standard sit and straddle sex position, the man sits on a chair. He will then stretch his legs out forward, for better balance (you'll find out later on why). You will then climb on top and lower yourself on him.

He will then hold your arms and you will lean back and hold on to him as well for better support. To get a better penetration angle and better leverage, you (the woman) will have to stretch your legs outward (Fig. 5).

Fig. 5 Galloping horse position

Pros

- This is another great position for guys who have smaller penises. But it also provides an ultimate entry for guys who are well endowed. You can feel her enveloping your cock through and through.

- The woman is in control of the pace while the guy just makes sure that his woman doesn't fall on the floor. It's a fair deal actually since both of you are working to get the deed done.

- Prepare for some of the biggest orgasms in your life due to the really deep penetration. It is a position for some really great G-spot action.

Cons

- It's a bit uncomfortable for the woman since she will have to keep her legs stretched out – and sometimes she has to keep her legs up in mid-air for that truly sensual angle.

- TIP: grab a pair of footstools so she can have somewhere to place her feet when she stretches them. That way she can also have some sort of base so she can rock back and forth a lot harder.

The Corridor Canoodle

This is a good sex position for couples who usually itch for a quickie. It's a great position if you live in a dorm or you frequently go to places where there are narrow corridors and hallways – you know where the walls are really close to one another. Now, why would you think that?

Well, you can find a dark empty hallway, lean back, lower your pants/skirt and get on with it. In this position, the girl can have it her way while the guy can enjoy some really deep and sensual penetrations.

How to Do It

The guy leans against one wall. He then shuffles down slowly until his feet can reach the wall on the other side. He anchors his back and feet there for support. After that, the couple can remove their lower garments (or just slip them down if they want to, so they can put them back on easily in case someone comes along from across the hall).

The woman then climbs on top and rides his man. The woman will have her legs dangling on either side of him. It's so easy just like riding a horse – only much more pleasurable (Fig. 6).

Fig. 6 Corridor canoodle

Pros

- Great for spontaneous out-of-this-world quickies (for those times when you just have to have him/her).

- Easy starts and quick orgasms

Cons

- The guy gets to carry the girl's entire weight on his legs (some muscle strength required there).

- You can get caught if you're not careful – but it does increase the excitement if you do it in public.

- The position is really tricky – may take some practice to get it done. A good place to practice is in the bathroom especially if the walls there are really narrow.

Intimate Sexy Spoons

As you might have guessed, this sex position is a slight variant of the spoons position. And just like the original, it's a great option for people who prefer a slower pace in the bedroom. You can use it as a relax mode after some heavy hard action.

How to Do It

The woman lies on her side with her knees bent. The man lies on his side as well behind her. He will then place his arm (the one on the bed, the one he's lying on) and position it underneath her neck.

The woman can use that arm as a pillow to support her head. That arm can be used to fondle her breasts and caress her front parts. He then enters her from behind and scoots his body closer to hers. He then does a rather slow in and out action as he plays with her breasts and maybe makes some soft pinches at her nipples.

The man can then use his free hand feel around her nether parts. This position is also great for some anal action but entering her maybe a bit of a challenge.

With a little practice, you can do some anal sex while your free hand can be used to stimulate her clit – thus mimicking a double penetration.

Tip: the woman can lean back a little against the man's body. She may even lay her leg (the one that is not in direct contact with the bed) on top of his thigh so she would open up a little bit, allowing better access.

Pros

- This is a very intimate position

- This position can be used either as a warm-up or as a position that you can transition to in case you want to relax a little bit after some really hot steamy sex

- This position also allows the man to really do his woman and give her pleasure from several points of contact at once.

- It also allows the couple to last longer in bed.

- It can pave the way for some really amazing and hot orgasms.

Cons

- It will be a bit difficult to perform especially for a man with a bulging beer barrel of a tummy.

- It is also not ideal for guys with shorter penises

- It is very easy for the penis to slip out in this position even if the guy is really well endowed.

- This position can be a bit awkward the first time you try it.

Chapter 5: Change of Scenery

If you really want to spice things up and impress your partner, ditch the bedroom scene. It is far too easy to fall into a rut of sex is that thing you do before rolling over and going to sleep at night. Mixing it up and making sex about, well sex, instead of about an activity that you are supposed to do can start with a quick change of scenery.

Throughout the House

Every room of the house is open to some sexual adventure.

The kitchen can be a great place to explore with food items and turn cooking into a whole new experience.

The living room may provide for some different positions that will truly drive your partner wild.

Go for the stairs if you want to get in some fun with soft ropes and ties or even just a new perspective.

Sex in the shower can bring on the steam in more ways than one. For a bonus, get a handheld massaging showerhead. The massaging jets can be incredibly stimulating.

Take it outside

However, don't be limited to what is within the confines of your home. Get really adventurous and take a turn in some of these different locations.

When was the last time you went to the "lookout point"? Find a nice quiet spot and see just how steamy you can make your car windows. Just watch out for the gear shift and make sure you have the emergency brake on!

What about skinny dipping? While it seems like something that just the kids do, bringing out your watery side can really ignite your passion and fuel an amazing sex life.

Camping out in nature might bring up thoughts of ants and bugs but when you look past that, the experience can be fun and different.

And don't forget the romp in the hay if you happen to be near a barn for this memorable experience.

A change of scenery isn't about what you do all the time. Instead, it is about introducing something new and different on occasion. You can't impress your partner if you are stuck in the same old rut.

Chapter 6: The Other "Naughty" Places

When most people think of sexual body parts, they naturally think of the breasts, the vagina, the penis, and sometimes the anus. With this mindset, it's natural to focus only on those parts of the body to stimulate a sexual response.

Fortunately, though, many other "naughty" places can be very sensual and often lead to significant arousal. By focusing on these other places, you will show your partner that you are multifaceted and know your way around their anatomy.

Let's talk about some of these and how you can make the most out of each area.

The Face

Whether it is the lips, eyebrows, or the ears, many people are highly aroused by a simple touch or a light massage in these areas. Maximize these locations by beginning foreplay while quietly cuddling on the couch in front of a movie. You can stroke or massage these areas without any indication of what might come next.

The Feet

While most women are not specifically turned on by having their men suck their toes, they certainly do give brownie points for a great foot massage. Taking the time to rub your partner's feet can help them to reduce their overall stress level and open them up to be ready for what might come next. This is part of what we talked about earlier in making sure that foreplay is all day.

The Legs

There are two places on both men and women that can be highly arousing.

First is behind the knees. The soft spot in the bend of a leg can often be very ticklish but it can also create a strong sensation that heightens the feelings in the groin region. Be sure not to take this too far as tickling can often be a turn-off if taken too far.

In addition to the knees, the thigh area can be highly erotic. Massage the muscles right up to where the legs meet the groin without actually touching the groin area. The closer you get, the more enticing this can be.

Men often think about going straight for the breasts and the vagina. To really impress your partner, avoid these areas until she is begging you to touch her there. Focus on the other naughty places first.

The Testicles

Women are often afraid to address a man's testicles for fear that they may end up hurting their partner. Don't be afraid to kiss, caress, or even lightly squeeze the testicles. Your partner will let you know if it is too much or just enough.

The Perineum

The perineum is the soft stretch of skin on a man between his testicles and his anus. This location is highly sensitive and can provide for heightened sexual intercourse. Stimulation can be a caress or light pressure.

The Anus

While you might not be ready for anal intercourse, the anus is full of nerve endings, and playing gently with this area is just one more way to explore your partner's sexuality. Even without penetration, using a finger or a vibrator to lightly rub or caress the anal opening can lead to intense sexual feelings. If you are feeling adventurous, consider using your tongue for this purpose.

There are many areas on the human body that are ripe for sensual stimulation. Explore all of them to determine how to best impress your partner.

Chapter 7: Sensual Massage

The sensual massage is about being fully present for your partner. The result does not have to lead to sexual intercourse but simply in providing your partner with a truly amazing experience that will entice them to feel better about their own body.

Preparation

To truly impress your partner when giving him or her sensual massage, be sure to prepare the room. While it seems cliché; candles, soft music, and soft lighting can significantly improve the atmosphere and results. Multitasking and providing a massage while catching up on a TV show is not going to provide for a memorable experience.

The Basic Sensual Massage

A typical sensual massage involves light touch all over the body focusing on points that will increase sexual energy such as the breasts, vagina, and penis. However, the focus of touching these areas during a sensual massage is less about stimulating to complete arousal and more about increasing your partner's awareness of these areas. The touch should almost be more of a tease and a bit of enticement.

The Energy Massage

Another type of sensual massage is an Energy Massage. In this form of massage, your partner is blindfolded and has on headphones with some relaxing music so there is some form of sensory deprivation in addition to the massage.

Once your partner is ready, the massage begins. However, unlike traditional massage that involves either light or heavy rubbing, a sensual energy massage consists of passing your hands over the various parts of the body without actually making a physical connection.

As you pass over each part of the body, stop and focus on sharing your energy with your partner. Feel the energy pass from your fingertips into their body at each point. You may choose to spend extra time focusing, but not touching, the specific areas of the body where energy is felt the strongest. These areas include the penis and vagina.

It is important to remember that the point of this massage is not to have sex. It is to have an experience with your partner that will allow you both to become more deeply connected.

It is best to perform each session independently rather than back to back. This isn't about taking turns but rather about being fully present for your partner's experience.

It may take a few times to master the art of the sensual energy massage but it can be a freeing and highly enjoyable activity while you are learning.

Chapter 8: Fantasy

Fantasy has a long and rich background in sexual history. The human mind is designed to be creative and part of that creativity is dreaming up new ideas about what sexual experiences may be fun and exciting.

Individuals are often afraid to share their sexual fantasies with their partners out of fear or shame. Creating an environment where your partner knows that they come first and are what you care about most will help them to open up to your fantasies as well as to be more willing to share their own.

Not all fantasies are meant to be fulfilled and dreams of a threesome with the model on a favorite magazine are usually not possible. However, there are a great many smaller fantasies that are very possible when openly shared and discussed with your partner.

How to Bring It Up

The hardest part about fantasy fulfillment maybe just bringing it up with your partner. It is usually not best to bring up a fantasy in the heat of the moment. Individuals often feel vulnerable and easily manipulated at these times. Have conversations around fantasies when you are both relaxed but not preparing to jump right into business.

Start with simple fantasies rather than jumping in with your deepest, darkest desires. This allows your partner to get used to the idea of something new and different and they may be much more open to using toys during sex than to a threesome with his or her best friend.

Remember that the best fantasies happen when both partners are willing participants. Not everyone is into the same stuff and some ideas may be a big turn off for others. Listen to one another and have an open discussion. If it doesn't fit for both, there should be no pressure to perform.

Your fantasies might involve role-playing or the use of unusual toys. You might be thinking about an exciting place or even a threesome. Be open to talking about what ideas you have and see where it may lead.

Chapter 9: A few Décor tweaks

I've said it over and over again and I'm going to repeat it – everyone is not the same. That can apply to our physical status, too. Sometimes, physical realities can get in the way of your good time. But there's an answer. There's always an answer!

Bodily discomfort is one of the major roadblocks to enjoying sexual pleasure. It can also get in the way of your woman's ability to reach orgasm. Back and neck pain can strike at any age. Injuries, stress, and strain can lead to chronic pain and make sex less enjoyable than it should be. After putting your time into reading this book, you don't want that. You want to make your honey as comfortable and relaxed as possible so she can enjoy the roaring waves or orgasmic pleasure you're going to share with her.

Using what you have available to achieve your partner's total comfort is one way to take action. Pillows and bolsters can be used to help get her in position and keep her comfortable while she's there. You can use these too. But nowadays, there's a whole range of useful and dare I say, intriguing, supportive aids that can help.

The tantra chair

Based on the classic erotic work, the Kama Sutra, this piece of furniture doesn't look like what it is. That way, when your mom comes over and sticks her head in the bedroom, she's not going to faint, right? What the heck, you can even put it in the living room and make it the little joke you and your partner have together at Thanksgiving dinner, with the whole family unwittingly chowing down on the turkey!

The Tantra Chair is an attractive piece of furniture and looks like a top designer might have created it. Classy and unobtrusive, its voluptuous curves will have your friends and family asking where ever you found such an unusual chaise longue. I guess that's what it is. It's just a chaise longue with a really fun, orgasm-inducing purpose. Oh yes. This baby is more than just a pretty chaise.

It's a chair specifically designed for you and her to make that sweet love on!

For those of you going the kinky way around, you'll be happy to hear that sex chairs and loungers are often equipped with hardware that will perfectly suit your newly acquired love for restraints! This can add a whole new dimension of fun to your elegant and unobtrusive sex furniture. Best of all, any fittings included can be removed when you have mom over, and "voila!" Your sex chair is now just a classy chair or chaise longue once again – for mom to sit on!

It even comes in different colors to match your (no doubt) classy décor. Its eco-friendly, stain and germ resistant, and best of all, guaranteed for a lifetime of love play. Makes a swell Christmas gift, too, for your discerning woman! Or your mom!

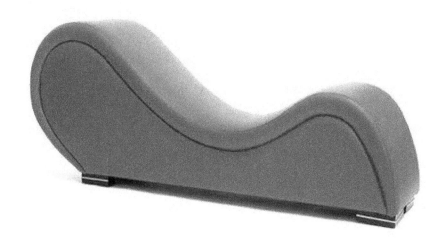

Love Bumpers

These ergonomically shaped cushions work the same way as a pillow might if you were to use it to elevate your woman's hips for lovemaking – only way better, because they're designed for this specific purpose.

They come in a variety of shapes that serve your sexual purposes in a very intentional way. These can be tucked under the bed, or stored in a closet. They also come in larger sizes that are more like the Tantra Chair, or a similar sex chaise. Covered in stain-resistant, antimicrobial fabric, these long-lasting daddy's little helpers will become some of mommy's best and most supportive friends. Love Bumpers are specifically designed to help place your woman's pelvis in exactly the right position to more easily achieve orgasm. You know she's going to love that!

Swings, slings, and Hammocks

Annnnnd back to the kink! Swings and slings are the wilder side of sex furniture, to be sure. Believe me, though; these décor tweaks can be a whole lot of fun for both of you. The way you use these is a matter of personal choice and preference, but swings and slings are designed for one of you (don't laugh until you've tried it, buddy) to be suspended from, while the other plays with the person hanging in it.

Swings and slings come in a variety of configurations. If you have a playroom (which you may have, or have someday soon, if you're the adventurous sort), a swing or sling can be a permanent fixture. If not, some models stand on a flexible frame or mount over a door.

The person in the sling is suspended from stirrups for the legs and buttocks. There's hardware for the placement of a variety of restraints, or you or your woman can hang place your wrists through the loops provided. Slings are made of a variety of materials, from neoprene to leather.

Slings also come in hammock styles, which allow the person suspended to recline in total comfort and safety and include head, hip, and shoulder support. There are also wooden and metal versions of these that are more like a hanging bench, which are padded for comfort.

When using any of these items, be sure to keep safety in mind. While they're a lot of fun, allowing the person suspended to completely relax and be attended to in the ideal position for sex, you must read the instructions. You need to ensure that any mounting structure can support the weight of the person suspended and that there's not going to be a nasty accident. You might have to explain that hole in the ceiling (if you mount your swing, sling, or hammock to it) to someone, eventually. You will not be able to blame the dog, I'm afraid.

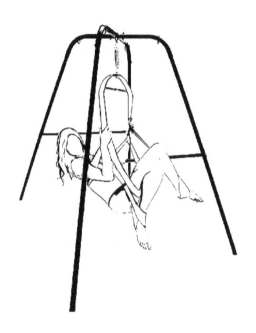

Chapter 10: Mr. Romance

We've taken a good look at all the factors that influence the ability of a woman to get to where she wants to go – the Big "O" – in the pages of this book. We've explored physiology, technique, props and toys, and lots of other fun stuff and some of the reasons that your woman needs you to be an Orgasm Master to make sure she's getting there.

Beyond all that, though, there's good, old-fashioned romance. It never goes out of style and women stop wanting it to be part of their sex lives. Women are naturally romantic. That doesn't mean some of us aren't, too. It just comes more naturally to the average woman than it does to the average man. Add to that our way of seeing the roles we're "supposed" to play and well, you know how it goes.

Like our emotional lives, our inner Prince Charming has been stunted by the story we're told about what men are supposed to be like. Again I say

"Bullshit!" Romance is fun and it pays off like the lottery in the bedroom. Take it from me.

Setting the scene

If you're not living with your woman, you're probably like most guys. You don't give an actual rat's ass about the way your place looks. There may even be car parts on the dining room table. Your bed will not only probably not be made; it will probably have a large dog lying in the middle of it, licking its balls.

No, dude. Not romantic. When your woman comes to your home and you want to seduce her like the Orgasmatronic love god you are, you need to clean up the home front. If you're not willing to do that, your woman should never see the inside of your home. I'm just being honest, here. Nothing turns a woman off quicker than stepping into a world of smelly socks, unmade beds, holey, stinky towels, and dirty dishes.

You can do way better than that. Start with clean. (Seriously, this is the minimum effort you should make). The bed, especially, should be made up with clean sheets, dog-free, and put in some semblance of order. There should be covers on the pillows. Vacuum the rugs. Wash the dishes. Make it look fit for human habitation, especially of the female variety.

Women like it when you make an effort. Cleanliness is the absolute minimum effort you should make if you're living solo and expecting your honey to come over for a night of love. You won't get far if your place is a nightmare vision of hell that looks like the herd from the Walking Dead just shambled through there.

But to set the scene for a night of fun with your woman, you need to do a little more. Whether you live together or apart, women love it when you make an effort to please their romantic natures. If you live together, surprise her when she gets home. Have the lights low. Have the candles lit and have the bath drawn. You can hold the rose petals. Nobody expects you to get that detailed.

Layout the sex toys. Pull down the covers and put on the music. Present her with a glass of wine, as she walks through the door. Be dressed, not to impress, but to appeal. You want her looking you up and down and thinking "yum", the minute she walks in the door. Look hot, my brothers.

You don't even have to cook; if that's something you suck at. If you suck at cooking, just don't. Order in! Make it something sensual, like Thai or Indian food. Something that's not too heavy, so you're primed for a night of erotic fun and not overstuffed.

Food as orgasm Booster

You can also think along the lines of aphrodisiacs. It's widely known that certain foods can up your libido and that's what you're going for.

Chilies, containing the chemical capsaicin, are known to get your blood moving and blood has a lot to do with arousal. Capsaicin also stimulates all those nerve endings you're hoping to get stimulated to help your woman get to the Land of "O". So whatever you choose, see if you can't add a little more fire (not that you don't have plenty already). BONUS: eating chilies helps you fight the battle of the bulge! Asparagus and avocado contain a healthy dose of Vitamin E. This vitamin assists your body and hers to produce all those delightful hormones, like testosterone and estrogen. Feeding her either of these delicious greens will boost swelling in the clitoris and also, vaginal secretions (and we like those, don't we, gentlemen?)

Pomegranates have always had a reputation for being a super sexy food item, but did you know why? These delicious, seed-filled balls of fun are loaded with antioxidants. These play an important part in the protection of your blood vessels and by now, you know how important those are to sex. When blood rushes to the genitals, arousal is heightened and pomegranates can help with that. Plus, they even look sexy!

Get Sensual

Sex is all about sensuality and scents are part of that. Even what we can't smell (but is definitely there) can get us revved up. Pheromones lead us to the one we desire like a silent siren song. But we can choose to heighten the mood that's already present in our chemical reaction to the women we love to love and hers to us, by adding some strategic olfactory stimulation.

We know women like candles and we know they like them scented. But some scents are just sexier than others and can actually stimulate both of you sexually. Like some foods, these scents are not only pleasant, but pack an erotic punch you can employ while setting the scene for your night of hot, orgasmic loving'!

Since the 18th Century, doctors have prescribed vanilla to men who want to be at their peak in bed. It's that powerful. For centuries, the scent has been used in perfumes by the Chinese, also. Why? Because they know how men respond to it. I think, to be honest, that's why women like it – even though they may not know why. We are talking Love Jones elixir and nothing less. It's also a mild euphoric, which will serve as a great prelude to the euphoria you're fixing to send your woman into.

Black licorice has been proven to be the most sexually stimulating scent for women. Add cucumber to that mix and you have the world's hottest combination for firing up your partner for a night of passion. Combining oils in a burner with these two scents is bound to get her roiling with desire before you even lay a finger on her.

Let the games begin

When you sit down to eat, focus on her. Trot out some of that dirty talk you've been working on and start massaging her mind into the kind of limpid, languid readiness it needs to be in for you to take her to the Land of "O". Tease her. Compliment her. Have fun. Pretend you're on your first date and you want her to like you. Maybe that's a role-playing game you can enjoy together on this special evening.

You may also want to do the dishes together, even if you have a dishwasher. Make it a sexy, fun event and another avenue of engaging in foreplay. Stand behind her, kissing her on the neck, or nibbling on her ear, as you scrub those dishes into the kind of lather you're sending her into. The dishes can drip dry tonight. You have other things to take care of – like you're now well warmed up woman.

The dance if Love

Whatever music you've chosen to be the soundtrack to your night of orgasmic seduction, I hope you've thought in terms of slow dancing with her to it. Choose it well. Make it sexy. Barry White is an old-timer, but damn that music gets women going.

Take her hand and lead her to an open space in the room. Look her in the eye as you draw her into your arms. Feel her melt like a stick of butter, as you slide your hands down her waist to her hips, then to the small of her back. Don't grab her ass just yet. That can wait.

It's a known and proven fact that women love to dance. You don't have to be dancing with the Stars material to make this one work for you. You can be the biggest, clumsiest ox in the world, but you can still go right-left-right-left in time to the music. If you can't, practice privately until you can. You want to feel that woman melting in your arms like candle wax, so you can meet her in others way, later. It's worth the effort, bro'. Trust me. Just do it.

After you've got her swooning from all the romance you're oozing, sit her down someplace comfy (where there's room for you to sit next to her later) with a glass of wine. Excuse yourself for "just a moment". Go and put the finishing touches on the love chamber.

Light the candles. Light the incense or scented oil (because sensual femininity loves the scent of anything delicious and this will only enhance her experience and yours). Now return to where you're seated your lover and get the party started. Sensual, fluid chat, punctuated by gentle nuzzling, pointed and gentle touching will soon turn to more sexual topics, as she is now practically a puddle on the floor. Before you know it, the two of you will be locked in a sensuous embrace and she will be ready for the kind of love you're well equipped to give her.

Romance isn't something you need to stage-managed every single time the two of you make love. But every so often, romance is a way to say you're putting a lot of thought into how much you enjoy seeing your woman up and how much you care about the quality of her experience and the intensity of her eventual orgasms.

There are plenty of times when all either of you will want is a lunchtime quickie. Maybe you'll want to go park somewhere and get to the point in the back seat of your car, the way most of us did in high school – or an elevator, or a stairwell, or the beach, or your parents' broom closet! Because you're now Agent Orgasm, you'll find that your woman's willingness to try new and exciting sexual adventures will be greatly expanded.

Having pried the lid off the cookie jar, the two of you are enjoying more, better, and more wildly varied sex than you ever thought possible, and all because you took the time to read this book and up your orgasmic IQ. Good going, buddy.

Chapter 11: A Little Bit Risqué

The Head Rush

This position requires the man to move to the edge of the bed with his upper body off of the bed and preferably resting on the floor. The woman then takes her position on top. This position is called the Head Rush because the extended length of time in this position will literally make the man's blood rush to his head, affecting a head rush. This could also refer to the case of blood rushing to both his "heads."

This position is also known by the friendlier and slightly deceptive moniker "Waterfall" (Fig. 7)

Fig 7 The head rush position

The Cowgirl

We've already discussed the woman on top position and explained how it differs in depth from the cowgirl.

The cowgirl requires the man to lie on his back while the woman goes on top of him using an upright seated position. Like the woman on top position, this allows for increased G-spot stimulation and more control over the amount of clitoral and vaginal stimulation for the woman.

For increased stimulation, the woman can employ a forward and backward rocking motion as well as circular gyrations to bring forth her orgasm. The satisfaction the man can get from this is the constant penile stimulation as well as a very erotic view of his partner as she controls her orgasm.

Some other tips to make this more enjoyable for both parties can include the man providing short upward thrusts to meet the woman's downward motions as well as the woman letting go of one arm or both for support and relying more on just the power of her leg muscles to perform the pelvic gyrations or rocking motions (Fig. 8).

Fig. 8 The cowgirl position

The Reverse Cowgirl

The reverse cowgirl gets its name for the simple reason that it is done in a slightly different manner as the cowgirl position. Instead of sitting upright facing her partner, the woman sits upright with her back towards her partner and performs the same motions as those of the cowgirl position.

This provides the man a very erotic view of the woman's backside and allows for different sensations though almost the same motions are employed.

This position is also called the Rodeo Drive and the Halfway around the World, but for the most part, it retains its more common name which is the Reverse Cowgirl.

This can be further modified by allowing the female to vary her angles from leaning forward or back and adjusting the amount of pressure as she pumps down. The man can also provide tactile stimulation by caressing the accessible portions of her vagina or her anus (Fig. 9).

Fig. 9 The reverse cowgirl

Face-Off

This is a very erotic sexual position and is done while sitting on a chair or the edge of the bed. The woman then sits facing the man and wraps her arms around his back and controls the level of intensity of thrusts by riding up and down the male shaft.

This allows for a lot of intimacy and is a very comfortable position that will allow long drawn-out sex sessions (Fig. 10).

Fig. 10 Face off position

The Hot Seat

This is the reverse of the Lap Dance or Face-Off position and can also be done by using either the edge of the bed or a chair. What this basically requires is for the man to sit on the edge of the bed and then allow the woman to sit on his member.

This is also known as The Love Seat and or The Man Chair.

The Pole Position

This is a slight variation of the reverse cowgirl but will require a little bit more effort from the man as he has to keep one leg outstretched in the air. The woman then assumes the position and grabs hold of the outstretched thigh as a means of dual support (Fig. 11).

This is also known as the Thigh master.

Fig. 11 The pole position

The One Up

Every woman's vagina and clitoris are unique. This therefore means that there are varying levels of sensitivity for women. This sexual position is targeted towards women who have a particular sensitivity to one side of their clitoris.

This requires having the woman lie on the edge of the bed with one leg rose supported by wrapping her hands around her hamstring just below the knee. This will allow her to have more control of her hip movements and it can assist you in locating the perfect spot to achieve maximum stimulation.

The Spider

This may sound a little bit complicated but is actually very easy to perform. What this will require is a little bit of choreography between you and your partner.

What this requires is for the man to sit on the bed with the woman seated on his lap. The partners face each other with arms back for support. Now here's the complicated part: you will have to move in time with each other thrusting forward, or you can rock back and forth in unison. This position allows for a very erotic view as the woman has her hips between the man's spread legs with her knees bent and feet outside of his hips. Both partners can maintain eye contact while they are performing this sexual act (Fig. 12).

This act is also called the Crab Walk.

Fig. 12 The spider position

Getting a Leg Up

This is a slight modification of the Crab Walk. Instead of the woman's legs spread out on the bed, she lifts these up onto the man's shoulders.

This can lead to very quick orgasms as the woman can control her pelvic movements easily (Fig. 13).

Fig. 13 getting a leg up

Bottoms Up

Are you up for a bit of a challenge? Well, here's one! The Bottom's up is a little bit difficult to perform as it requires a little bit of contortionism and athleticism. First, the woman lies on her back and the man straddles her as she is facing away. Next, she lifts her legs to wrap them around his back and at the same time to elevate her pelvic region for easy entry. Last, she then grabs on to the man's buttocks and, with a concerted effort, slides up and back.

You'll have to try it to find out just how pleasurable it is! (fig. 14).

Fig. 14 Bottom up position

Sidewinder

The man and the woman lie on their sides facing each other. Spreading her legs, the woman allows the man to enter her. In this position, the couple can see each other and this encourages a lot of physical contact like hugging and kissing.

This is also called the facing spoon.

The Horny Mantis

This is a variation of the sidewinder. While in the sidewinder position, the female lifts her leg up and over her partner's body and locks he in place by securing her leg on the man's back. This position allows for deeper penetrations.

The Standing Dragon

This move is a modified doggy style where the man has to stand while the woman gets on all fours at the edge of the bed. She will have to spread out a little bit more than usual and arch her buttocks more for this position.

Entering from behind, the man gets a very erotic view of her buttocks as he pounds into the woman. Thrusting in this position can be done lightly or as aggressively as the woman wants.

Another fun name for this is the Crouching Tiger, Hidden Serpent (Fig. 15).

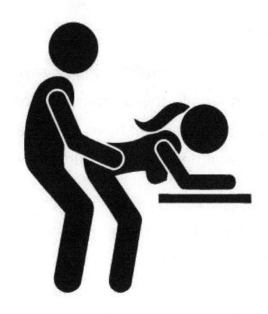

Fig. 15 The standing dragon

The X Position

The X position is basically what its name portrays. It will require you and your partner to lie facing each other with your legs forward and over on top of each other. This forms an X, hence the name.

This position is a bit limiting so thrusting is instead replaced with small gyrations that prolong arousal and lead to great orgasms.

Wheelbarrow, Standing (The Hoover Maneuver)

Everyone knows that sex burns calories but the wheelbarrow has to be credited as one of the sex positions that can really give you a workout!

The man enters the woman from behind and then lifts up her legs and locks these in place by his waist. Now, the couple can stroll around the house while at the same time having sex and burning calories (Fig. 16).

Give it a try. It's good for a laugh or two!

Fig. 16 Wheelbarrow position

Seated Wheelbarrow

This is basically the same as the wheelbarrow but only this time, the man is sitting down on the edge of the bed or a chair. It is a bit less strenuous and absurd but still provides the same sexual benefits.

Scissors

The couple lies opposite each other with their legs pointing towards each other. The woman lifts one leg up while the man enters at a 90-degree angle forming an x. the man will need to maneuver his penis at a downward angle to enter the woman's vagina.

It sounds complicated but once you do it, you'll find it's pretty simple.

The Pillow Driver

When the missionary position gets a bit old, why not incorporate a little workout in it to rejuvenate the act?

Tilt her pelvis up by shoving a small pillow under her lower back or buttocks. This allows for an upward angle which will give you more control over the direction of your thrusts.

Since this is a variation of the missionary position, you'll have to support your full weight by bracing yourself with your arms outstretched as if doing a pushup. While you lower yourself, let your pelvis thrust into her and change the angle of the thrusts every now and then.

The CAT

Before you think that this is an allusion to a sexy cat, the CAT is actually an acronym for Coital Alignment Technique. This is the best position for women who find it hard to achieve orgasm through sexual penetration.

What this basically requires is for the man to assume the missionary position with his body further up and to one side. This means the man's chest is going to be near either her right or her left shoulder. The next thing to do is have the woman bend her legs at a 45-degree angle and then tilt her legs up.

This position allows for constant contact between the clitoris and the man's pelvis.

If your woman is finding it hard to reach orgasm, do this and she'll thank you for her entire lifetime! (Fig. 17).

Fig. 17 The CAT position

The Pushup

The pushup is a modified missionary position as it requires the man to fully rest his weight on his arms. This position requires the man to be physically fit to perform this.

This is also called the mountain climber because of the intense workout the man can get from this.

Quick Fix

This is a standing doggy style position as the woman bends at the waist and rests her hands on some furniture, her knees, or the floor for support. The man then enters from behind and holds on to the woman's hips for support as he thrusts.

Tactile stimulation can be done simultaneously while performing this position.

This is also called the Bends for obvious reasons.

The Ballet Dancer

This is a very erotic position that can be done in very tight spaces. The woman raises one leg up and then wraps it around the man's buttocks or thigh and then penetration occurs. The man can also assist the woman as this position can get tiring by cradling her raised leg.

A woman may raise her leg up and over the man's shoulders if she is flexible enough (Fig. 18).

Fig. 18 The ballet dancer position

Belly Flop

Have your woman lie down on the bed with her back towards you, her hips raised, and her knees bent slightly. Place a pillow under her and then enter from behind while at the same time propping yourself off of her with your arms.

The Anvil

Do you know why this is called the Anvil? If you picture the penis as a hammer and imagine the amount of thrust generated through this position, you'll get the idea.

This position requires the woman to lie on her back as the man kneels between her legs and raises them. Next, he rests her calves onto his shoulders and drives his penis into her.

This position allows for very deep penetration and may be uncomfortable for the woman so remember to exercise caution. It is always a good thing to allow for short thrusts at first to allow the vagina to get accustomed to the deep invasion (Fig. 19).

Fig. 19 Anvil position

The Pretzel

Are you ready for a twister? This position requires a little bit of contortionism.

First, the man has to kneel and at the same time straddling the woman's raised leg as she is lying on one side. She then bends her other leg around the man's waist and gives him access to her vagina.

In this position, you can complement your pelvic movements with manual stimulation of her clitoris (Fig. 20).

Fig. 20 The pretzel position

The Lazy Man

The lazy man is a great way to allow your woman to take control of the situation and pace. This requires sitting on the bed with pillows behind your back for support. The woman then lowers herself onto the man's penis and straddles his waist while planting her feet flat firmly on the bed. She can then dictate the manner and speed at which she wants to achieve orgasm through her movements.

You can even transition from this move to the Crab Walk or the X Position. The key is to experiment with this very basic position and have fun! (Fig. 21).

Fig. 21 The lazy man position

Conclusion

There was quite a bit of information to take in, so don't worry if you feel a little overwhelmed right now. Sex is a real part of life, and talking about sex is not always comfortable − and talking about a bunch of different sex positions? That can be even more difficult, especially if you read this book because you need to add a little zest to your life after dark.

The fact is that keeping the fire burning bright beneath your sex life is not always easy. This is especially true if you are a part of a long-term couple. Over the years, as we talked about, life just gets in the way. It becomes easier and easier to forget to focus on the sexual part of your life as a couple. The next thing you know, the two of you are more like roommates than lovers. Fortunately, it is never too late to improve your sex life. That is what this book is for − making your sex life EXPLODES! This book has given you all of the knowledge you need to get started on improving every aspect of your sex life, as well as start to embrace your sexual nature. After all, we are all only human − and we all have a sexual side to our beings, one that wants to come out and play.

This has been a long book. It has been a lot of chapters with a lot of information to take in. But every piece of information is going to help you and your partner come together, both literally and figuratively. Your sex life is simply too important to your overall happiness to pretend that it is okay – because "okay" sex is not the kind of sex you or anyone else wants to have. Sex starts as a learning experience, and it will always be a learning experience. The next step after accepting the fact that you will always have more to learn about having great sex is simple – you need to START having great sex! Pick a chapter, pick a position, and let your partner know that he is in for a treat tonight – or later today, whenever you want to do it.

Remember, this book is just the beginning for you. Great sex is part of living your very best life. This book teaches you the path to making the absolute most out of your sex life. It is up to you to start walking down that path, and keep walking down that path – hand-in-hand with your partner or on your own. Sex IS natural, sex IS good, and sex IS something that everybody should do if given the chance.